LATITUDE & LONGITUDE
Geography 2nd Grade for Kids
Children's Earth Sciences
Books Edition

BABY PROFESSOR

EDUCATION KIDS

Speedy Publishing LLC
40 E. Main St. #1156
Newark, DE 19711
www.speedypublishing.com

Latitude and longitude refers to a system of imaginary east-west and north-south lines on the earth.

They measure how far north or south an object is on the Earth.

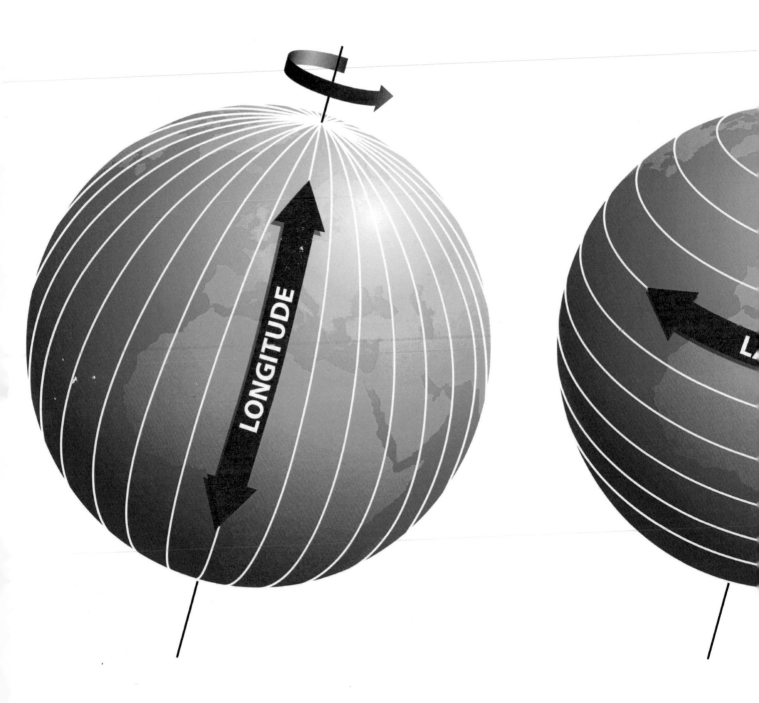

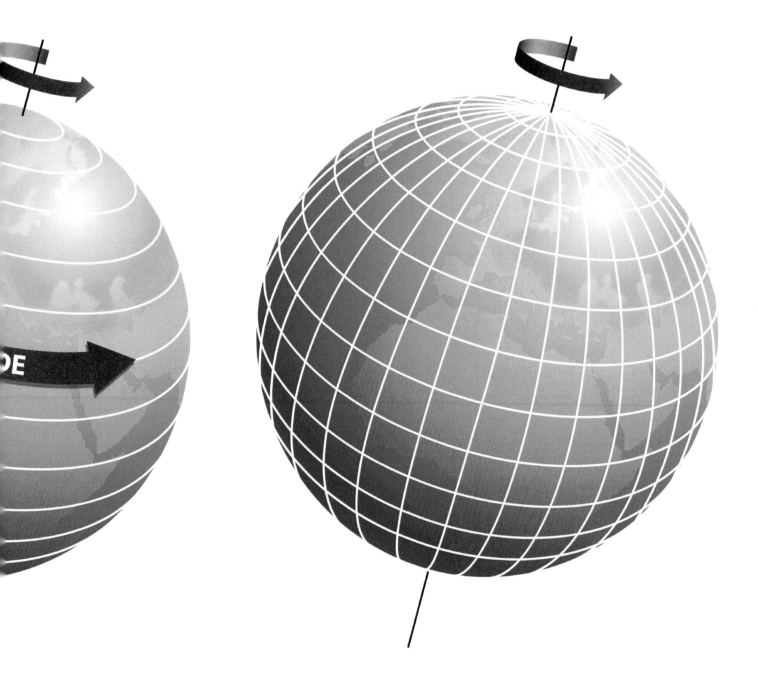

This grid of intersecting lines on a globe enables us to identify every location on earth with a set of numbers or letters.

It is commonly called
a grid system.

Екватор

Північний тропік

-20°

Latitude is the angular distance, in degrees, minutes, and seconds of a point north or south of the Equator.

Lines of latitude
are often referred
to as parallels.

Lines of Latitude are called parallels because the lines run in the same direction as the equator.

The Equator is an imaginary circle around Earth. It runs east and west halfway between the North and South poles.

OCEANUS

ÆTHIOPICVS

TROPICVS

Fig. II.

MERIDIONALIS

CIRCVLVS

VTERIOR
Monoc Mugi

G VINE

IN-
FERIOR

MVMBIR

CAFRE

RIA

Melinde

I. S. Mathei

I. Annobon

Angoy I.

Cap Nigro

Port S. Ambre
Pr. Sierra

Pr. das
Voltas

Sin. Saldaone
Sin. Mont Tabularis
caput Bonæ Spei

I. de Tristan
I. de Alvares

Cap Terræ Aust
Terræ de vue

I. S. Hilena

I. de Mauritii

Tanchere
Prom.

S. Roman

I. Dina

I. Marseveen

Cap Circoncision

I. Nachtig

Tolus

OCEANVS

ÆTHIOPIS

ÆTHIOPIA

AFRICA

CAFRE

Cap. al Nolumbio

The latitude at the equator is 0°.

If we move either up or down from the equator, our distance increases, and so does our angle to it.

Even though latitude is always measured and expressed in degrees, it is easily converted into miles.

The distance from
the equator to either
pole is 6,222 miles.

Longitude is the angular distance, in degrees, minutes, and seconds, of a point east or west of the Prime Meridian.

Lines of longitude are often referred to as meridians.

Meridian comes from
the Latin word which
means "midday".

The sun crosses
each meridian in the
middle point between
sunrise and sunset.

As meridians, move away from the equator, they come closer together until they meet at the poles.

The poles have no longitude because all meridians meet there.

Did you enjoy reading this book? Share this to your friends.

Visit

BABY PROFESSOR
EDUCATION KIDS

www.BabyProfessorBooks.com

to download Free Baby Professor eBooks
and view our catalog of new and exciting
Children's Books

49301462R20025

Made in the USA
Middletown, DE
12 October 2017